THE ONE-EYED PEOPLE EATER
THE STORY OF CYCLOPS

by Joan Holub
illustrated by Dani Jones

Ready-to-Read

Simon Spotlight

New York   London   Toronto   Sydney   New Delhi

Dear kids,

Long ago, Greeks wrote stories called myths. These stories helped them to understand things that were happening in the world around them. Myths also taught lessons about right and wrong. Some characters in mythology do things that are impossibly amazing or flat-out wrong to help teach us what *not* to do in real life!

—J. H.

SIMON SPOTLIGHT
An imprint of Simon & Schuster Children's Publishing Division
1230 Avenue of the Americas, New York, New York 10020
Text copyright © 2014 Joan Holub
Illustrations copyright © 2014 Dani Jones
SIMON SPOTLIGHT, READY-TO-READ, and colophon are registered trademarks of Simon & Schuster, Inc.
For information about special discounts for bulk purchases, please contact Simon & Schuster Special Sales at
1-866-506-1949 or business@simonandschuster.com.
The Simon & Schuster Speakers Bureau can bring authors to your live event. For more information or to book
an event contact the Simon & Schuster Speakers Bureau at 1-866-248-3049 or visit our website at
www.simonspeakers.com.
Manufactured in the United States of America 0114 LAK
First Edition
2 4 6 8 10 9 7 5 3 1
Library of Congress Cataloging-in-Publication Data
Holub, Joan.
The one-eyed people-eater : the story of Cyclops / by Joan Holub ; illustrated by Dani Jones. — First edition.
pages cm. — (Ready-to-read)
Summary: An easy-to-read retelling of the Greek myth of the Cyclops, who traps Odysseus and his friends and
threatens to eat them.
1. Cyclopes (Greek mythology)—Juvenile fiction. [1. Cyclopes (Greek mythology)—Fiction.
2. Mythology, Greek—Fiction.] I. Jones, Dani, 1983- illustrator. II. Title.
PZ7.H7427One 2014
[E]—dc23
2013004552
ISBN 978-1-4424-8500-6 (pbk)
ISBN 978-1-4424-8501-3 (hc)
ISBN 978-1-4424-8502-0 (eBook)

CONTENTS

CHAPTER 1:
SHIPWRECKED

There once lived a happy Greek king named Odysseus (oh-DISS-ee-us). He was happy because he and his army were sailing home to Greece.

They had fought the Trojan War in another country for ten years. They had finally won. Now Odysseus could hardly wait to see his family again.

On the trip home it began to rain. Lightning flashed across the sky. Huge waves tossed Odysseus's ship this way and that. They were soon shipwrecked on a nearby island.

Odysseus and his men were hungry after fighting the storm. But they had no food to eat. They only had grape juice. Odysseus picked up a bottle of juice.

"Let's go see who lives on this island," he said.

"Maybe someone will trade us milk and cheese for our juice."

He and twelve of his men went in search of food.

Soon they found a cave. They went inside to look around. There was food everywhere! Dinner was cooking in a big pot.

"I wonder who owns all this?" said Odysseus.

"Let's take some food and leave before the owner comes back," suggested his men.

"No," said Odysseus. "Let's wait and ask the owner. I'm sure he will be glad to share."

CHAPTER 2:
TRAPPED

Stomp! Stomp! Stomp!

In walked a giant.

He was big. He was hairy. And he had only one eye! It was right in the middle of his forehead. A herd of sheep followed him inside. Then the giant pushed a heavy rock in front of the cave's opening. Odysseus and his men were trapped!

The giant stared at the men with his one big eye.

"I am Cyclops (SI-klops)," he said in a grumpy voice. "Who are you and what do you want?"

Odysseus was scared, but he tried not to show it.

"We are hungry travelers. We were hoping to share your dinner," he replied.

"I am always glad to have visitors for dinner," Cyclops said.

Suddenly he grabbed two of the sailors. He tossed them into the air. He opened his mouth wide. The men fell right in.

Crunch! Crunch!

Cyclops gobbled them down.

"Get it?" he said. "Visitors *for* my dinner? *Ha! Ha! Ha!*"

The men didn't laugh. They were angry and scared. Cyclops didn't care. He went to sleep. Odysseus and his men could not move the rock at the door. There was no escape!

CHAPTER 3: THE PLAN

The next morning Cyclops woke up hungry.

"Where is my breakfast?" he asked in his grumpy voice.

He grabbed two more men.

"Oh! Here it is!"

Crunch! Crunch!

He gobbled them both down.

"See you later," he told Odysseus.

Cyclops moved the heavy rock from the cave's doorway. He took his sheep outside. Then he pushed the rock back into place. Odysseus and his men were still trapped!

"We are all doomed," groaned Odysseus's men. "He will eat the rest of us when he gets back."

"Don't worry. I have a plan," said Odysseus.

He found a long stick in the cave. It was as big as a tree trunk. He and his men cut one end with a knife until it was pointed and sharp. Then the men hid the stick.

"When Cyclops comes home, we will be ready," said Odysseus.

That night Cyclops returned.
Stomp! Stomp! Stomp!
He grabbed two more men and gobbled them down. This made Odysseus very mad. But he hid his anger.

"Would you like a drink?" he asked
Cyclops.

"Sure, why not?" said Cyclops.

Odysseus gave him a cup of grape juice.
Cyclops took a sip.

"Yum. This is good."

Cyclops drank more and more. The sweet
juice made him sleepy.

24

CHAPTER 4:
THE TRICK

Cyclops looked at Odysseus with his one sleepy eyeball.

"What is your name?" Cyclops asked.

Odysseus decided to trick him.

"My name is Nobody," he said.

"I will reward you for giving me some juice, Nobody," said Cyclops. "Your reward is that—I will eat you last!"

"Thanks a lot," said Odysseus.

But Cyclops didn't hear. He was snoring away.

Odysseus and his men got the sharp stick from its hiding place. They leaped on Cyclops's belly. He didn't wake up.

"One. Two. *Three!*" said Odysseus.

They gave a big push. They stuck the sharp stick into Cyclops's eye.

"Owww!" Cyclops roared. "You poked me in the eye!"

Cyclops swung his arms back and forth. "Just wait until I find you. Then you will be sorry."

But he could not catch the men because he could not see them.

Cyclops felt his way to the door. He pushed the heavy rock out of the way.

"Help me!" he yelled.

Soon his neighbors came running. They were all Cyclops, too!

"What's wrong?" they asked.

"Nobody poked my eye with a stick!" said
Cyclops. "Help me catch him."

"You want us to help you catch nobody?"
his neighbors asked. "That does not make
any sense."

They all went back home.

Cyclops sat down so he blocked the cave doorway.

"You will never get away," he told Odysseus. "If you try to leave, I will grab you and gobble you up."

"Don't worry," Odysseus whispered to his men. "I have a new plan. An escape plan."

CHAPTER 5: THE ESCAPE

When the sun rose, Cyclops called his sheep.

"Time for you to go outside and eat some grass," he told them.

As each sheep passed, Cyclops felt its back.

"I will not let you escape by riding my sheep outside," he told Odysseus.

Luckily Cyclops did not think of feeling the sheep's tummies. Because that is where Odysseus's men were hiding. Odysseus had tied the sheep together in groups of three. Under each middle sheep, he had tied one of his men. All six of his men were soon safely outside.

But now Odysseus had a problem. There was no one left to tie him to a sheep. So he grabbed the underside of the last sheep and hung on. Little did he know that this sheep was Cyclops's favorite pet!

As the last sheep passed by, Cyclops petted its back. Odysseus held his breath. Would Cyclops find him?

"You are usually the first one out," Cyclops said to the sheep.

"I guess you are sad and slow today because I am hurt."

He gave the sheep a hug. Then it ran outside taking Odysseus with it. Odysseus was free!

CHAPTER 6:
THE LESSON

Odysseus and his men returned to their ship and sailed away. They looked back at Cyclops. He was still sitting in his cave.

"We have escaped!" Odysseus shouted at him.

"And we have taken some of your sheep. Maybe that will teach you to be nicer to visitors next time."

Cyclops roared in anger. He picked up a
giant rock and threw it.
Splash!

It just missed Odysseus's ship. The splash made a big wave that gave the ship a push-off.

"Thanks for the boost!" yelled Odysseus.

He and his crew sailed toward home once again.

As for Cyclops—he did not change his ways. To this day he is still his same old grumpy self. So don't ever visit him around dinnertime, if you know what's good for you!